THE WAY WE THINK WHAT WE ARE

WHAT ARE YOU?

MOHD FAISAL DAD KHAN

Xpress Publishing
An imprint of Notion Press

XpressPublishing
An imprint of Notion Press

Old No. 38, New No. 6
McNichols Road, Chetpet
Chennai - 600 031

First Published by Notion Press 2019
Copyright © Mohd Faisal Dad Khan 2019
All Rights Reserved.

ISBN 978-1-64760-445-5

I thank my parents for supporting me all the time...

Everything i am today and everything i may become tomorrow is all for the sacrifices my parents made for me. A big thank you for all the moms and dads in the world.

God has blessed me in so many ways, but the biggest of them all is my parents. They deserve the best from me always. Thank you to my parents!

I may not always say how much I love both of you but I can say I have a big place in my heart only for you two. Thank you, mom and dad, for raising me so perfectly!

Thank you for not only being a parent to me but also being a teacher and a mentor. You are the reason for all the successes in my life!

Being a parent is difficult, even more difficult is being a friend to your child. I'm lucky that you were both my parent and a friend! Thank you!

I didn't have an awesome childhood because I have awesome friends. I have an awesome childhood because I have awesome parents. Thank you mom and dad.

Dear mom and dad, I have let so many years pass without thanking you both. But you haven't let a single second pass without loving me unconditionally.

Contents

Contents

Foreword

Faithless To be yourself in a world that is constantly trying to make you something else is the greatest accomplishment.

Preface

"Begining of working times are tougher than the time you will get in future to take rest"

-Mohd Faisal Dad Khan

1. The Way I Feel What I Can Be

Sometimes i think what if i didn't wake up someday?

What people will say about me?

What people will think about me?

I don't know what they are saying or what they thinking about me.

People will forget once you left. No one will remember your presence

Life is all about thinking and being what we are.

I believe it's important that we are always fully ourselves, even if it means we don't fit in with other people, because when we are not truly ourselves it is impossible for us to be happy. It is impossible for us to be fulfilled.

So when you're hanging with people that you really don't fit with, and you get that feeling deep down, that's your inner self telling you, you're not comfortable, which means you're not happy, so it's super important, that we are always, always, fully ourselves. Be true to you.

2. Get out of your head and into your heart...

Do the things that make you light up! Do the things that make you forget to check your phone. More of the things that make you smile, MORE of the things that make you laugh like a little kid! MORE of the things that make YOU proud to be YOU!

Be BRAVE! You only get one shot at this life. One opportunity to LIVE FULLY. One opportunity to create some MAGIC.

It's ok to say no sometimes. To say no with PASSION. With authentic certainty because you know what is best for you!

Not everyone will get it, and that's ok. The right people will walk the path with you and most won't be able to resist… because someone who is GENUINELY, who is authentically loving life, doing EXACTLY what they want to do…. that person is infectious!

Real passion is infectious! Wake up with passion every day!

Wake up EVERY SINGLE DAY and be NO ONE but FULLY, 100% YOU!

I believe it's important we go for everything we want in life because we only have one life to live
So we have to give it everything we've got and try to make our dreams, our hopes, our aspirations become reality.

3. You Are Unique

All of us have looked at others and wished we could be like them. We wished we could have what they have.

But you can't be someone else. You are you. You are unique and have your own talents and experiences. You can use those talents and experiences to get what you want, but you shouldn't sacrifice yourself to do so.

Many of us also act like someone we are not. Whether you did it to impress a love interest, your boss, or someone else, we have all not been ourselves because we believed it would get us what we wanted.

But when you are not yourself, you change. You change who you are and what you are about. You change your thoughts and beliefs and you become someone who tries to please others instead of pleasing yourself. You become someone else instead of being yourself.

Being yourself does not mean you are selfish and it doesn't mean you don't care about others. Being yourself means you like who you are. Being yourself means living life how you want to live it, regardless of other people's opinions. And it means you respect yourself.

Don't worry about what others think. You can't control them or their thoughts.

If you like who you are, then that is all that matters. Don't allow others to change who you are. You are being judged regardless of what you do, so being yourself makes happiness easier to obtain.

Being yourself is important because you will not be happy otherwise. Empower and love yourself.

Unless you can be a unicorn. Then be a unicorn.

Chapter 4

The ability to believe in yourself can change your life.

Just think:

What difference would it make in your life if you had an absolutely unshakable confidence in your ability to achieve anything you really put your mind to?

What would you want and wish and hope for?

What would you dare to dream if you believed in yourself with such deep conviction that you had no fears of failure whatsoever?

5. How To Believe In Yourself

Most people start off with little or low self-confidence, but as a result of their own efforts, they become bold and brave and outgoing. And we've discovered that if you do the same things that other self-confident men and women do, you, too, will experience the same feelings and get the same results.

The key is to be true to yourself, to be true to the very best that is in you, and to live your life consistent with your highest values and aspirations. This is the only way to truly learn how to believe in yourself.

Take some time to think about who you are and what you believe in and what is important to you.

If you want to change your life by becoming an author, believe that you can do it. The hardest step in that journey is finding the confidence to learn how to write a book. Once you get a hold of a proven system to plan, produce, and publish your work, the larger goal becomes easier to attain.

By believing in yourself, you will find the courage to take immediate action on your goals. And this, as you may know, is the key to success!

I encourage you to never compromise your integrity by trying to be or say or feel something that is not true for you.

And – more importantly – never compromise your potential to grow due to self-limiting doubts. Instead, embrace your confidence and believe in yourself because you really can do anything you put your mind to.

6. Tell Yourself You Have Confidence And Believe It

Repeat affirmations such as "I believe in myself" every day.

Your thoughts become words and your words become your actions. If you continue to tell yourself that you believe in yourself, eventually you really will believe in yourself.

It's that simple.

Have the courage to accept yourself as you really are—not as you might be, or as someone else thinks you should be—and know that, taking everything into consideration, you are a pretty good person.

After all, we all have our own talents, skills, and abilities that make us extraordinary.

No one, including yourself, has any idea of your capabilities or of what you might ultimately do or become. Perhaps the hardest thing to do in life is to accept how extraordinary you really can be, believe in yourself, and then to incorporate this awareness into your attitude and personality.

7. Believe In YourSelf

• 25 •

Everything seems impossible until we try...

Your values in life determine your beliefs, about yourself and the world around you.

If you have positive values, such as love, compassion, and generosity, you will believe that people in your world are deserving of these values and you will treat them accordingly. When you believe in yourself and chose to be a good person you will find yourself to be more positive and successful in life.

8. Set Expectations And Know Your Value

Your beliefs, in turn, determine the third ring of your personality, your expectations. If you have positive values, you will believe yourself to be a good person.

If you believe in yourself to be a good person, you will expect good things to happen to you. If you expect good things to happen to you, you will be positive cheerful, and future-oriented. You will look for the good in other people and situations.

9. Expect Good Things To Happen

The fourth level of your personality, determined by your expectations, is your attitude. Your attitude will be an outward manifestation or reflection of your values, beliefs, and expectations.

For example, if your value is that this is a good world to live in and your belief is that you are going to be very successful in life, you will expect that everything that happens to you is helping you in some way. As a result, you will have a positive mental attitude toward other people and they will respond positively toward you.

You will be a more cheerful and optimistic person. You will be someone who others want to work with and for, buy from and sell to, and generally help to be more successful.

10. Be A Good Person

The fifth ring, or level of life, is your actions. Your actions on the outside will ultimately be a reflection of your innermost values, beliefs, and expectations on the inside. This is why what you achieve in life and work will be determined more by what is going on inside of you than by any other factor.

10. Wanting to be someone else is a waste of person you are

I know that sometimes it can be hard to be yourself. I know you might get scared of what other people think. So do i. I mean don't we all? But either way, it does not mean you have to pretend to be someone you are not. People judge. That's Life. If they don't like who you are then so be it. That's their problem. So the best you can do is be yourself and don't pretend. Its better than not having people get to know the REAL you. I have friends and i also HAD friends. The real friends are those who think that you are who you can be and i am so lucky to have these friends in my life.

My friends are different from others because they never let me think that i can't and that's the thing which keeps us together.

I don't know why they do it but still, they believe that i can do, i can be my self.

Love you friends and thank you for being a part of my life...

11. Yourself

I can't think of a more powerful source of motivation than a cause you care about. Such cause can inspire you to give your best even in the face of difficulties. It can make you do seemingly impossible things.

While other causes could inspire you temporarily, a cause that matters to you can inspire you indefinitely. It's a spring of motivation that will never dry. Whenever you think that you run out of motivation, you can always come to your cause to get a fresh dose of motivation.

Your cause is a powerful source of motivation but it's still abstract in nature. You need to make it concrete in the form of a dream. Imagine how the world will be in the future. Imagine how people will live and work.

Having a dream is important because it's difficult to be motivated if you don't have anything to shoot for. Just think about people who play basketball. Will they be motivated to play if there is no basket to aim at? I don't think so. They need a goal. You need a goal. That's what your dream is for.

But just having a dream is insufficient. Your dream must be big enough to inspire you. It must be realistic but challenging. It must stretch your ability beyond your comfort zone.

We have all heard the saying "good things take time."

While true, how many of us are able to adopt this concept in our day to day
lives?

When a baby is born, we don't rush it into becoming a toddler. When we
plant a rose, we don't complain to the seed while it takes it's time to grow
and strengthen before becoming a plant and eventually blooming.

So why do we not adopt the same gentleness with our lives?

12. Faith

When we have faith in God, The Universe or a power that is greater than ourselves, it becomes far easier to allow things to unfold in our lives.

With faith, comes trust.

Having faith does not then mean that we do not honour the need for control in the aspect of our lives where it serves us.

What it does mean is that the pressure that has been created internally for you can release, you can finally breathe a little deeper into your belly and accept the natural ebb and flow of life.

Learning to expand your life and your experience without pressure is not about putting more pressure on yourself! It's about accepting that perhaps your current standard of living needs to shift and taking responsibility to change it.

If today was your last day….

Did you do all you can do?

If today was your last day….

Did your life matter?

You don't know when your time is

Don't leave your dreams dying

Leave your legacy shining

You owe it to yourself

One day it will, will be all over

Don't keep regrets, when you get older

Live your life full,

Keep moving forward

Make sure you live before it's over

Our thoughts help shape our reality, and that's why thinking thoughts of limitlessness is so important. One useful technique to switch your limiting thoughts to limitless ones is to hit the CONTROL + ALT + DELETE button on them. You can even say "CONTROL + ALT + DELETE" out loud or to yourself whenever you notice an idea that no longer serves your best interest coming into your head. Then simply replace it with one that does serve you well.

The key here is to have a positive thought handy so that you can quickly reshape your ideas about your future. Our minds are like children who will go back to doing what we told them not to do unless we redirect them to something better. That's why it's so beneficial to listen to affirmations and motivational speakers – they not only make you feel better in the moment, but their underlying message of empowerment also becomes part of your automatic response to life's challenges.

14. People Won't Tell

• 41 •

There are many aspects of our identities that it is simply hard for us to see without the help of another person. We need others to be our mirrors, feeding back their insights and perspectives on the elusive, hard-to-see parts of ourselves.

However, getting hold of data from others is a very unreliable process. Very few people can be bothered to undertake the arduous task of giving us feedback.

Either they dislike us too much and therefore can't be bothered. Or they like us too much, and don't want to upset us.

Our friends are too polite; good intentions lead them to keep their less pleasant observations to themselves. Our enemies have so much to tell us: it's not always the people we like who see certain aspects of us most clearly. It might be someone we're at loggerheads with who has the sharpest sense of what's not quite going right in our character (a way, for instance, of letting people down after a long period of seeming to go along with their plans; a very annoying habit of sitting on the fence). But they are not likely to be good at sharing their wisdom with us. They either won't take the trouble, or will brush us off with the sort of sharp insults that will make us defensive and closed to the wiser aspects embedded within their harsh assessments.

15. perseverance

They say life doesn't give you what you deserve but what you fight for. Life has all that we need to live like gold underneath the earth that you need to extract from the mother earth.In extracting it there levels of difficulties which we encounter. As we go deeper the earth there level that is soft and others are rocky and hard which makes one to give up but one thing as an individual on a journey you need to understand that every level needs a different approach or strategy. Encountering rocky and situations in life doesn't mean you should give up.In the journey of life or moving with your vision, you need to demonstrate perseverance, not giving up easily because you never know that one hit that hardy and rocky situation there is that precious gold, that breakthrough which you desire. I have realized that a lot of people give up on the verge success or breakthrough. Giving up must not an option in one's life. All people who had achieved their desires possessed a greater hunger for fulfilment than of giving up.Imagine if all inventors of the things that we see in this world lacked perseverance, this world would be like amazon forest.In my life, the level of my mistakes and failures can not be compared the insatiable desire to live a mark in this world and a great foundation for the next generation.I will persevere no matter how long it takes.At the present moment, i can qualify for highest qualification in this world in terms of failing but i will not give up.Greatest valleys or gouges were created through persistence.

16. Worth of living

You will get so many situations in your life but not every situation is going to stay for long.

Some people quit their jobs because they think they can't.

But the people who think they can are the only one who can defeat any problem.

Some will quit because they lose someone who they loved a lot but the people who think that they will get better than that not now but in their future will get much better than their expectations.

People will do suicides because of some stress, force or any situation that they cannot express.

Why we use to write etc at the end of our answer in our examination booklet, you should know one thing that it is not et cetera it is "End Of Thinking Capacity"

17. Importance

Do you remember the last time you spoke to your mother? If you do, when was that? Do you remember the last time you expressed how much you love her? If so, when?

I am unsure if it was only me but we tend to have this habit of shying away from the expressing how important our mother or our father to us.

I don't know why people shy saying that they love their parents. Take a moment to think that how they raised you by efforts and how did they paid your fees to make you an educated person.

Give them a time to see your face, give them a time to hear your voice, give them a time to say you something...

We are too busy to ask our parents that are they happy by seeing us this much busy and not even a minute of time we have to ask them and tell them that we love them...

We all learnt one thing just by hearing it from others or from any other source that "Give Respect Take and Respect" but we don't know that if we want respect then we should respect our parents first.

18. At Last

Love yourself, accept yourself, forgive yourself, and be good to yourself, because without you the rest of us are without a source of many wonderful things.

Getting ahead in a difficult profession — singing, acting, writing, whatever — requires avid faith in yourself. You must be able to sustain yourself against staggering blows and unfair reversals. When I started thinking that I'm me and i can be me forever, and yet I never let my desire slide away from me, my belief in myself and what I felt I could achieve.

THE END

Wants To Thanks My Friends

Is it their ability to laugh with me (and sometimes at me) for hours on end?
Or that they'll be there for me at a drop of a hat if i need a shoulder to cry on?
Or the fact that they love me unconditionally for everything that I'm (and i ain't)?

Having great friends to share your life with is a gift like no other…

After all, friends are the family I've chosen.

"Friendship is born at that moment when one person says to another: 'What! You too? I thought I was the only one."

Want to thanks my friends Ahmed, Austin, Mustafa, Samar And Shafi for being a part of me and for making me feel like i can do it, especially for that moment when i was at the point of thought to be i can't…

Whenever I needed someone to listen to my problems, you were there, whenever I needed to express myself, you were there.

I was never tired of this life and It is not gonna matter if I fall down twice, coz I know each time I fall you won't let me hit the ground.

Thanks for being a part of my life.

Bernard M. Baruch

"Be who you are and say what you feel, because those who mind don't matter, and those who matter don't mind."

— Bernard M. Baruch

"तुम कौन हो और कहते हो कि तुम क्या महसूस करते हो, क्योंकि जो मन के लिए मायने नहीं रखते, और जो मायने रखते हैं वे बुरा नहीं मानते."

— बर्नार्ड एम। बारूच

Copyright